Praise for *Honest, Direct, Respectful*

"Dennis Adams has captured the essence of management and interpersonal relationships with his simple message of Honest, Direct, and Respectful communication (HDR). We have instilled this message as part of our corporate culture by adding it to our vision statement. Our staff consistently says that they use HDR in their personal lives as well."

JACK HORN, CEO/EXECUTIVE DIRECTOR
PARTNERSHIP HEALTHPLAN OF CALIFORNIA

"I have been using Dennis Adams' extremely practical HDR process for over seven years. I constantly coach up-and-coming managers with this model; now all of my managers use the Honest, Direct, and Respectful terminology and approach as a norm, which has led to new levels of trust within our team and to improved satisfaction for our customers."

GREG CHRISTIAN, OPERATIONS SUPPORT LEADER
KAISER PERMANENTE TRI-CENTRAL SERVICE AREA,
CALIFORNIA

"Dennis Adams' approach to communication style is promising, personal and productive. It demonstrates direct, straightforward communication and in itself is honest, direct and respectful. It is a map for improved interpersonal skills that go beyond simple communication. I believe individuals and organizations that embrace this approach will find it to be a plus sign in a life-changing experience."

ROBERT L. DOCTER, PH.D.
PROFESSOR EMERITUS, EDUCATIONAL AND
COUNSELING PSYCHOLOGY—
CALIFORNIA STATE UNIVERSITY, NORTHRIDGE

Honest, Direct, Respectful addresses fundamental differences in communication styles and provides a clear pathway to improved personal and professional communication. It is a 'must have' for any business leader."

JOHN GUYER
PRESIDENT & CEO
NEXSYS

Honest
Direct
Respectful

Three simple words that will
change your life

DENNIS D. ADAMS
with Sue Schumann Warner

VMI PUBLISHERS
Sisters, OR

VMI PUBLISHERS

Sisters, Oregon

www.vmipublishers.com

ISBN: 9781933204291

Library of Congress Control Number: 2006936592

Printed in the United States of America

Cover and graphic design by Joe Bailen

Contents

Dedication

his book is dedicated to Betty Lou and Bill Adams, who happen to be my parents. Although as a child I didn't understand the magnitude of their unfailing love, I can clearly see how self-sacrificing and loving they were—not only to me and my siblings, but also to many who were lost in this world and looking for a refuge.

Dad taught me the importance of being optimistic. He saw the obstacles in life as opportunities to trust God and move forward. He woke up early each morning, and prayed for his family and others. Even during difficult days I

7

can remember hearing him whistle, and I'd think to myself that everything was going to be all right. He is an individual of emotion and reason and has truly modeled the full scope of what it means to be a "real man."

Mom passed away several years ago and I truly hope she understood how important she has been to me. Although small in stature, she was very large in her personal presence. We would talk for hours about family and life, and she encouraged my softer side. Mom saw something in me that I didn't see in myself; she is the reason I do the work I do today. We could talk about everything, and her unconditional love and support helped me through many difficult times. She taught me that God could take the worst situation and turn it in to something "good." I miss her.

Thanks, Mom and Dad.

Introduction

My epiphany came during our weekly staff meeting, after having to sit through my boss' slide show from his summer vacation; we had gathered for business and ended up enduring two hours of family photos. As soon as the slides were over and the lights went back on, Bob (my boss) turned to us and said, "Well, how did you like it?"

"Wow!" I exclaimed. "It was really nice."

My friend Carl, who was sitting across from me, was a little more honest. "We could have gone there and back in the time it took you to show those slides," he said.

Bob was offended and walked out of the room.

Carl looked over at me and said, "You know, you're a kiss-up."

"Well," I replied, "you're rude."

I went back to my office and, for the first time, really questioned my communication style.

How about *you*? Have you ever questioned *your* communication style? Once I started paying attention to mine, I wondered, usually after I'd made a mess of things, "Why did I say *that*?" Or, "There I go again—I said the wrong thing, at the wrong time. *Again*." Or, "Will I *ever* be able to talk to that person without blowing up?"

Somehow, what I said was not what I wanted or intended.

At other times, I didn't say anything at *all*, I just walked away saying, "I wish I'd said...I should have said..." Obviously, none of us are born with perfect communication skills. While having the best intentions, I found I sometimes spoke in ways that hurt people; at times, I even found myself withholding the truth as a means of trying *not* to hurt people.

I just didn't get it.

I didn't realize I could learn to speak the truth honestly, directly and respectfully—saying exactly what I meant—and so live at peace with myself and those in my life: my spouse, children, neighbors, co-workers, my employer... (I even learned to speak effectively with those who I wished *weren't* in my life!)

In the pages that follow, I'll share my journey with you as a husband, father, therapist, mediator and minister, as I came to learn the value of being honest, direct, and respectful.

As we travel together through these chapters, *Honest, Direct and Respectful...Three*

Simple Words That Will Change Your Life will help you:

- understand your communication "style" or personality type—a short, self-test will show if you tend to be passive or reactive, or a "TOP"—a "ticked-off passive."
- discover the ways in which experiences from the past, such as hurt, anger and bitterness, affect how you communicate today.
- incorporate three simple words into your life—*Honest, Direct, Respectful*—and use them as a "filter" to measure your conversations.
- communicate effectively with anyone, anywhere, and at any time…by being honest, direct, and respectful.

Remember those words: they will change your communication style—and your life—forever!

What's Your Style?

We all have our own unique communication style, which for most of us is either *passive*—quiet and reticent, or even silent or unresponsive; or *reactive*—loud and aggressive or demanding and "in your face."

Remember my friend Carl, who called me a kiss-up after that slide show? When that happened, I realized I didn't like the passive person that I was—but I didn't want to be as rude as he was. My problem: I didn't know where to find the "center" or middle ground between being a kiss-up and being rude; in fact, I didn't even know there *was* a center.

I only knew that my passive communication style was making my life miserable.

Do you know what *your* style is? Here are some clues...

A passive person thinks like this:

- I feel bad, I don't want you to know I feel bad, I don't want to rock the boat.
- I don't like conflict.
- Why cause problems? I probably can't change the outcome anyway.
- I really want you to like me...therefore I'm not going to tell you what I really think or how I'm feeling.
- I don't want to make a mistake.

What does a reactive person think like?

- I feel bad, I don't deserve to have this bad feeling, I think I'll take a couple of people down with me.
- I'm upset and angry, and I'm not going to feel upset and angry alone. I'm going to bring you into it by making you feel as bad as I do.
- It's not important that you hear me, it's important that you see things my way.
- I often blow off steam because it "lets it out" and makes me feel better.

Communication Styles

(Continuum between passive and reactive)

Honest

Direct

Respectful

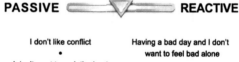

PASSIVE   *Center*   **REACTIVE**

I don't like conflict	Having a bad day and I don't want to feel bad alone
•	•
I don't want to rock the boat	Blow off steam and let it out so I can feel better
•	•
Why cause problems?	
•	I want you to see things "my way"
I'll give in for the sake of peace and harmony	

WHAT'S YOUR STYLE?

By looking at passive and reactive as a continuum, it's easy to see the goal wasn't for me to be more reactive, it was to move to the center—to be Honest, Direct, and Respectful—and the goal for reactive people is not to be more passive, but likewise to move to the center.

MAKING IT WORK FOR YOU...

Take the self-test on the following pages to help determine your communication style.

Style of Communication Indicator

This is a quick and simple way (non-scientific) to determine your natural style when dealing with difficult people and circumstances. When you answer, think of how you respond in **public situations**. By answering T (true) you are indicating this statement is **true** most of the time. When answering F (false) you are indicating this statement is **false** most of the time. Please answer all questions T or F. Being totally honest about what is mostly true and false will help you determine your communication style.

If you want validation, give this indicator to a few friends and family members and ask them to rate you.

1. _F_____ I almost always avoid conflict when I can.

2. _T_____ I sometimes hurt others' feelings without intending to do so.

3. _T_____ I often blow off steam because it "lets it out" and makes me feel better.

4. _T_____ I often have a conversation in my head about what others will think or how they will respond to me if I say what I am thinking.

5. _F_____ I often walk away from a conversation saying to myself or others, "I wish I had said…"

6. _T_____ I don't have any problem letting someone know that I'm upset.

7. _F_____ My family tells me that I act with more intensity at home than I do in public.

8. _T_____ It is difficult for me to remain silent in public when I have strong opinions.

9. _F_____ I have no problem "telling it like it is."

10. _F_____ I feel anxious when others are upset with me.

11. _F_____ Although I have a long fuse, I do blow up at times or engage in self-destructive behaviors.

12. _T_____ Others see me as a "peacemaker."

13. _T_____ I am very direct in the way I communicate.

14. _T_____ I have difficulty being honest if I think what I say may hurt someone's feelings.

15. _T_____ I don't like to "beat around the bush" when I have something to say.

16. _T_____ It bothers me when others don't say what they really mean.

17. _F_____ I get upset quickly and get over it in the same way.

18. _F_____ It is difficult for me to speak up in public even if I have a strong opinion.

19. _F_____ I don't get mad; I just get even.

20. _F_____ Others see me as soft-spoken.

(Check the next page to evaluate your style.)

Evaluation of Communication Style Indicator

1) Total the number of true answers for questions:
1, 4, 5, 7, 10, 11, 12, 14, 18, 20___3___(Passive)

2) Total the number of true answers for questions:
2, 3, 6, 8, 9, 13, 15, 16, 17, 19___7___(Reactive)

3) On the continuum below circle the numbers reflecting your total Passive and Reactive answers.

P ——————————————————————— R

10 9 8 7 6 5 4 ③ 2 1   1 2 3 4 5 6 ⑦ 8 9 10

- A higher total in **P** and a lower total in **R** indicates a passive style.
- A higher total in **R** and a lower total in **P** indicates a reactive style.
- A higher total in **P** and a high total in **R** (not as high as P) indicates a passive style; you're

probably not totally satisfied with the way you deal with difficult situations and people.

- A higher total in **R** and a high total in **P** (not as high as R) indicates a reactive style; you're probably not totally satisfied with the way you deal with difficult situations and people.
- Equal totals in the center is the sign of an Honest, Direct and Respectful (HDR) communicator. Is this mostly true? If so—great. For validation, ask someone else to rate you.
- Equal scores at both extremes means you are probably confused or haven't spent much time thinking about your style of communication.

As you can see from this test, people are passive or reactive in varying degrees. Keep this in mind as we explore these communication traits in subsequent chapters.

The 80/20 Rule (my observation)

In my years of clinical practice.

I've observed that about 80 percent of

the population is passive and

20 percent is reactive.

Are You a Passive?

During a corporate speaking engagement, I separated the managers from the rest of the attendees. There were about 25 in all, and I asked them to divide themselves into "passives" and "reactives" based on their own self-evaluation. They divided into about 80/20, passives/reactives.

I noticed one woman join the reactive side who had, the day before, told me she thought she was a passive. I said to her, "I'm a little confused; yesterday you told me you were a passive."

She looked at me and said, "There weren't that many reactives, and I felt bad for them." (A typical passive, people–pleaser response.)

We all laughed, and she went to the other side.

I then asked the reactive managers, "Is there something you want to say to the passive managers?" They said "yes," and proceeded to voice concerns like: "Why can't you be more up-front? We're sick and tired of you talking behind our backs. Why can't you say what you want to say? If you have a problem, why can't you put it on the table, and we'll talk through it?" They went on for about five minutes and then stopped, and seemed to feel a great deal of relief.

Next, I turned to the passive managers and asked if they'd like to respond. They said "yes"—and proceeded to turned to each other and talk about the reactive managers, saying things like, "I wish they could be nicer, why are they so loud? Why are they so angry?"

They didn't talk **to** the reactive managers, they talked **about** them.

—

How can you tell if you're a truly passive person?

1. Passive people dialogue in their head about "what happens next."
They can go through the whole process about "If I say this, they'll say that…they'll act that way…" and then they'll get to the end and say, "You know what, it's just not worth it!" Passive folks make good soap opera writers—they can keep this process going on forever.

2. If 100 people like you and one doesn't, your focus will be on the one who doesn't.
I've often thought of myself as a bull dog, hanging on to someone and saying "You **will** like me! I'll make you like me!"

3. You will avoid conflict at all cost.

This might be grounded in family history or you might just be a peacemaking type of person who sees it as a virtue. I was a minister for 11 years; I've struggled in this area because I saw it as evidence of spirituality and humility. But in reality, as I studied the life of Jesus, I found he really "lived in" the center. He was honest, direct, and respectful. Yes, he did react in the Temple (when he overthrew the money changers' tables) for example, and because it was not normal behavior for him, the impact was greater than if he behaved that way all the time. He also remained silent or passive at times, when it was appropriate. For example, when he was on trial before his crucifixion he chose to be passive, because no one was interested in his answers—they just wanted to convict him.

4. You feel you have to ask everyone else if they think you are passive or reactive.

You think you are passive, but feel you have to "check in" with others to confirm it. A good indication that you're passive: others' opinions are more important to you than your own. You become a mirror, only reflecting how others see you.

5. People accuse you of being manipulative, or tell you to "say what you really want to say."

It really bothered me when people called me manipulative. But I had to finally recognize that was the only way I knew how to get what I wanted. I would try to get what I wanted, or say what I wanted, but I was never direct, because I didn't want to hurt someone's feelings.

6. *You decide "I can't change the outcome, so it's not worth it" and so the outcome determines how you'll handle the problem.*

If you don't perceive the outcome to be positive, you say it's not worth it. In reality, when you learn to speak from the center, you'll find it's at least worth it to **you** and opens the potential for productive communication.

Actually, the only outcome passive people are worried about is how the other person will respond. But, when you learn to come from the center place, it will not only affect how you feel about yourself, but it can effect a more positive outcome.

7. *Passive people usually don't know what they want or need; even when they do know what they want, they are often afraid to say it.*

An example: two people are in car, and one asks, "Where do you want to eat?" the other one doesn't have a suggestion—they say they don't know. But, if alone, they would have no problem deciding where to eat.

8. *Passive people don't talk to people, they talk about people.*

Passive Cycle

TENSION / ANGER / STRESS

LIKED
BUT NOT
RESPECTED

PASSIVE
RESPONSE

DO NOT SHARE FEELING OR
THOUGHTS - ONLY WITH
SAFE PERSON

When passives react

A common misconception is that passive people don't react.

They do—they just do it slower than reactive folks.

I found I'd have a cycle where I'd fill up with tension or anger, and then I'd react. When I reacted, it felt great for the moment; later, I'd feel bad and think that reacting wasn't very good and I'd go back to being passive.

It's important to understand this cycle when you're trying to decide where you fall on the continuum between passive and reactive. It's easy to become confused! The question is, where do you naturally go first—to passive or reactive?

Passive/Reactive Cycle

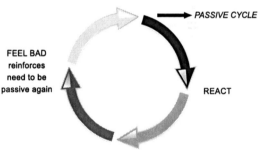

HONEST—DIRECT—RESPECTFUL

The Dilemma:

If I'm passive most of the time and then react, I'm only convincing myself that it's better to stay passive. If I learn to come from the center, I experience over time that I'm able to release the tension that particular events create, and I open the door to honest, direct and respectful inter-action with others.

Given a choice, passive people will usually choose

being liked over being respected.

MAKING IT WORK FOR YOU...

1. Think about your passivity
    - How has it worked for you?
    - How has it worked against you?
    - How motivated are you to find the center?

2. Think about an important passive person in your life. What behavior patterns did you learn from him or her?

3. Identify a time recently when you were passive. What alternative did you have in this situation?

What If You're a Reactive?

remember a co-worker—a woman who was
prone to speaking loudly and with great
intensity—who said, "People don't listen to
me at our team meetings."

I told her, "I have a thought about that,
would you like to hear it?" (by the way, this is
an Honest, Direct and Respectful skill)

She said "Yes."

I asked her, "Have you ever seen me angry
at a meeting?" She said yes, one time—and
she actually remembered the event. (This is an
important point. If I do have to come from a
reactive place from time to time—say, my

grandson is running into the street and I have to warn him to stop, because a car is coming—it can be appropriate.)

"It's not that a measured reaction is never appropriate," I told her, "but if you use reactivity all the time, **people will focus on how you're talking, not what you're saying.**"

She replied, "That makes a lot of sense."

I said, "Let's do something different at the next meeting: lower the intensity and volume of what you have to say."

When it came her time to share, everyone sat back in their chairs and got ready to tune her out. But when she started speaking, she lowered her voice. People couldn't hear her, so they all leaned forward.

That was the good thing; the bad thing was that she and I were laughing so hard, we couldn't continue the meeting. But the point was made.

If you ask a truly reactive person "How did you feel when you reacted?" you will receive one of these two responses:

1. *"What reaction? What are you talking about?"*

or

2. *"I felt fine, what's your point?"*

So, it's possible to be reactive and not know it. Remember, if 80% of the population is passive, they're certainly not going to speak up and tell anyone, "I think you are reactive!"

If a reactive person is aware of his or her style, they may feel some sense of guilt, yet not know where the center between passive and reactive is, or how to get there. When they do get to the center, they may feel naked—and be afraid they'll somehow be taken advantage of.

<u>Reactive Cycle</u>

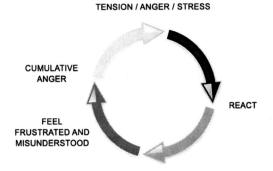

One couple put it this way: The passive spouse said, "If you just treat people nicely, you could get them to *like* you."

The reactive spouse replied, "Yeah—but if you give people an inch, they'll take a mile."

And that's the conflict in many of the relationships between passive and reactive people.

How to know if you're reactive

1. *Reactive people are more concerned with "winning," or being in the power position.*

It's not important that you hear me, it's important that you see things my way.

2. *If, as a reactive, you are having a bad day, you want everyone to know it.*

You probably want to make sure the people around you feel bad too, although you might not be aware of it. People stay away from you so they are not pulled into your "black hole."

41

3. Reactive people have trouble with communicating in almost all aspects of their life.
They'll often say, "I just blow off steam and then I'm over it." They don't let the anger and tension build up. While they might say, "I feel better," in reality they've mowed down anyone who came into their path.

4. If you're reactive, you're not aware of the effect you have on others.

5. Reactive people feel others don't understand them.

6. Reactive people don't trust—which makes sense, because 80% of the people (that's the percentage of passives) aren't telling them the truth.

7. Many reactives gravitate toward passive people; they tend to have an entourage of them.
This helps passive people feel protected and makes the reactives feel validated.

On the other hand, some reactives seek other reactives for reinforcement.

Moving to the center

One of the questions I ask my workshop participants is, "Who do you think goes to the center (the middle ground) easier?" The typical response: passives. (They're *so* nice, you know!)

In reality, reactive folks come to the center easier. Reactives usually say, "That makes a lot of sense. What do I need to do?" And the first thing to tell them is, *"You need to lower your intensity."*

Why? Because the intensity of your communication forces people to focus on your delivery and not what you're saying.

Reactive people aren't looking to be liked or respected—

they'd rather win.

HONEST–DIRECT–RESPECTFUL

MAKING IT WORK FOR YOU...

1. Think about your reactivity
   - How has it worked for you?
   - How has it worked against you?
   - How motivated are you to find the center?

2. Think about an important reactive person in your life. What behavior *patterns* did you learn from him or her?

3. Identify a time this week when you were reactive. What alternative did you have in this situation?

4

Maybe You're a TOP

One day, a woman was brought to me by her co-workers; she seemed very upset and they thought she needed someone to talk to. The woman sat down and I asked, "What happened?" She answered, "Someone came and took a pencil off my desk."

I asked, "What did you do?"

She replied, "I stood up in the middle of the room, shaking, and yelled, 'YOU TOOK MY PENCIL!'"

I said, "That's an interesting response."

Right away I could tell that this was a passive person who had let tension build up and was exploding for the first time.

She later told me that for the past seven or eight years, people had been either taking things off of her desk or moving items around on her desk. I asked if she had ever said anything when that happened, and she said, "No, I never did—today was the first day."

I asked, "Do you think they heard you?"

"No," she said. "They think I'm crazy."

So, she recognized that her passivity didn't work, but she didn't know where the center was, so she let it all out. She told me it felt good at the time, but afterwards she was embarrassed.

She experienced the same kind of epiphany that I did after I watched that slide show.

I told her she was a "TOP."

If you are still not certain if you are passive or reactive, you may be a TOP.

For many years, I thought people were only passive or reactive. Now, I've come to see that there are people who look reactive—but in reality are passive by nature.

This realization came about one morning in the middle of an assertiveness class I was taking in an attempt to break out of my passive bent.

The instructor talked about different communication techniques—being assertive or confrontational—and most of the discussion seemed to focus on the confrontational aspect.

At one point, I wrote on my notes "TOP."

A classmate noticed and asked, "What's that?"

I said, "That's who's teaching this class—a Ticked-off Passive."

This professor *looked* like a reactive person, but the more he talked, the more I realized he was a ticked-off passive—he had been passive so long, he was now angry at the world and was

47

teaching the students how to do what he wanted to do: 'tell people off.'

How to know if you're a TOP

1. You were passive for many years when you were younger.
Your passive nature worked for you for many years; people see you as nice, and they like being around you. As you get older, you realize it doesn't work well for you. You get angry and upset, and feel used and abused and you want to change that. You are reactive only to people close to you. For many years my family bore the brunt of the thoughts and feelings I didn't express to others. I would react at home, instead of coming from the center place and being honest, direct and respectful.

2. You feel horrible after you react (or know some-thing is not right).
Truly reactive people don't have that feeling. If you're a TOP, you feel bad about your reactivity, but you embrace it because it's the only way you know how to protect yourself.

3. You don't like being reactive but you don't want to go back to being a doormat.
At some point you say, "I'm here because it's the only choice I see. I don't see the center, I only see the two extremes."

4. You have little respect for passive people.
You feel resentful toward passives, because you know what they are doing—they're talking about you, because they don't have the courage to speak up—and you are judgmental toward them. You don't like it because it reminds you of who you used to be.

5. You start losing friends.
When you were passive you had a lot of friends, but when you turned into a TOP, people began to distance themselves from you.

6. People start saying things like, "You've changed."
You are aware you've changed, but you're defensive about it. You've moved to the only place you know, because you think: "I only know how to control or be controlled." So you try to take control by being reactive and going to the TOP place, instead of going to the center—the center being the honest, direct and respectful place.

7. You feel frustrated and angry most of the time.
Your anger isn't a release of tension; it creates more stress for you.

8. You appear to be a Dr. Jekyl and Mr. Hyde.
Keep in mind, a truly reactive person doesn't usually feel bad when they react. A TOP appears reactive, but their behavior makes them feel bad.

TOP Cycle

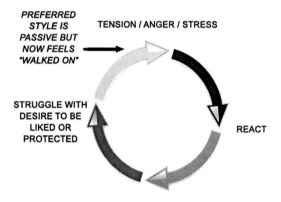

PREFERRED STYLE IS PASSIVE BUT NOW FEELS "WALKED ON"

TENSION / ANGER / STRESS

REACT

FEELS BAD BUT JUSTIFIED

STRUGGLE WITH DESIRE TO BE LIKED OR PROTECTED

Underneath, a TOP is a fed-up, frustrated passive

MAKING IT WORK FOR YOU...

1. Many times, passive people are mistaken for reactives. This is because they have become TOPs over time. If you are passive by nature, think of some of your TOP experiences. Have they increased through the years?

2. Think about the last time you acted in a TOP way. How did you feel? What led you to this reaction?

3. How has being a TOP helped you? How has it hurt you? How could you move to the center?

Moving to the Center

I have a brother who is reactive by nature. He called late one night and started chewing me out, giving it to me up one side and down the other. I finally asked, "Can we talk about this tomorrow?"

He said, "OK."

We got together for lunch the next day and began talking about the phone call. I said, "Let me ask you a question. Last night when you called, were you honest with me?"

"Yes, I was!" he said. And, he had been.

"Were you direct?" I asked him.

"Yes, I was!" he said. And, he had been.

"Were you respectful?"

"Well, I have a little trouble with that one," he admitted, "but I thought you could take it." (He only knew me as a passive person.)

I replied, "I know you did." Then I said, "You have to understand—if you call me and talk to me that way again, two things will happen: first of all, you'll jeopardize our relationship. And secondly, I'm going to hang up, because I don't deserve to be talked to that way."

His eyes got very wide. As a passive brother, I usually beat around the bush, maybe trying to shame or humiliate him. I had never been that direct without being angry.

Then, I asked him: "Was I just honest with you?"

"Yes, you were," he said.

"Was I direct?"

"Yes, you were," he agreed.

"Was I respectful?"

"You were."

I looked at him—and this is where some of the life-changing aspects of HDR come in—and said, "I learned to be honest and direct by watching you. I always admired those qualities in you. Maybe that's why I always seemed to be attracted to reactive people, although I never understood why. But you could learn to be respectful by watching me."

He called me a few months later and told me our conversation had made a huge impact on his life.

Now that we've looked at passive and reactive styles *and* TOP characteristics, let's see how we can use our understanding of these to move to the center, or middle ground, where we can begin to relate to others in an honest, direct and respectful way—and in doing so communicate effectively.

HONEST–DIRECT–RESPECTFUL

First, let's think about how passives and reactives measure up to being **honest, direct and respectful (HDR)**.

How Passives measure up to HDR

Is a passive person *honest*? (I'm speaking in communication terms only.) No, they're not usually honest about what they feel or think.

Is a passive person *direct*? No, they're not really direct.

Are they *respectful*? They usually do act respectfully, although they may not be respecting themselves.

So, passive people have one of the characteristics of HDR: they are generally *respectful*. This is an important attribute.

MOVING TO THE CENTER

How Reactives measure up to HDR

Is a reactive person *honest*? Initially, I thought so, and then I realized—based on working with thousands of reactive people during my career as a counselor and minister—there are two types of reactive people: those who are totally honest, and those who exaggerate. The ones who exaggerate may say, "Everybody in this department hates you," when only 80% of the people dislike you. What they do have is the *directness*. They are very direct, as their body language and presentation demonstrate.

Are they *respectful*? Usually, they're not—and they understand this when I show them the following model.

How Passive/Reactive Measure up to HDR

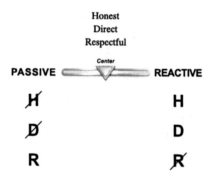

The HDR model

Moving to the center means making a conscious decision to use what I call the Honest, Direct and Respectful model. It sounds simple; while it's not easy at first, it gives you guidelines for measuring the dynamics in conversations.

How do you measure? By asking yourself if what you are saying lines up with *being honest, being direct, and being respectful.*

HDR Cycle

TENSION / ANGER / STRESS

FEEL RESPECTED BY SELF AND OTHERS

CHOOSE HDR

GAIN SENSE OF STRENGTH AND INTERNAL RESOLUTION

Moving to the Center

Once you understand what your style is—if you're a passive, reactive, or TOP—you can make a conscious decision to move to the center, and by doing so, you will learn to set appropriate limits and boundaries. If you move to the center, you will say, "I'm not going to allow people to treat me this way." On the other hand, I can't control them and I have come from what I now call a **place of strength, meaning I conducted myself in an adult manner** (That's an internal quality; I can only control myself, not others; I am only responsible for my own reaction and not another's.)

You must choose to move to the center; it's a process. It takes time.

HDR Model

PASSIVE ⟨══════ Center ══════⟩ **REACTIVE**

Honest

Direct

Respectful

HDR skills aren't about winning, confronting or controlling.

They are about coming from a

"place of strength."

MAKING IT WORK FOR YOU...

1. Think about HDR...
   —What is your strongest attribute?
   —What is your weakest?

2. How would you have to change your thinking/beliefs to move to the center?

3. Think of someone you know who is consistently in the center. What are some of their characteristics?

6

HDR—What Does It Mean?

I was the keynote speaker at a pharmacy conference attended by 200 people. Probably 190 of them were interested in what I was talking about, which was stress in the workplace. Sitting at a table in the back of the room were 10 people who were having a great time talking to each other. It was really distracting—especially if you're a passive person by nature, like me.

Now, I could have handled their disturbance in a number of ways: as a passive, I could ignore it and walk away; if I were reactive, I could give them a piece of my mind.

I decided to use a technique of silence—I folded my hands and stopped talking. As that happened, the room got quieter and 50-60 people turned to look at the people at the back table, who quickly stopped talking. As soon as I started speaking again, they started talking as well and got even louder.

Well, I finished my speech and then had to deal with my feelings about the table of talkers. Being passive by nature, my inclination was to ignore it. But, I was really very angry and distracted by it. I started to walk out, and then decided I had to do what I encouraged others to do: be honest, direct and respectful.

My first thought? To tell the director I would never speak to his group again. But, while that would be honest, it wasn't direct. He wasn't part of the problem. And, although I could have done it in a respectful way, I took a look at the check I had just received, and thought how stupid that would be.

I put the check in my pocket and walked

toward the back of the room, where the people were still sitting. Talking to them wasn't easy; my heart started pounding, and my voice was three pitches higher than normal out of nervousness. The group immediately covered their bases and said they really liked the seminar.

Then I said, "Can I chat with you folks? I want you to know it was extremely distracting when you were talking during my seminar. When I paused and looked at you—and you continued to talk—I was frustrated and upset. I hope you don't treat other speakers like you treated me tonight."

And I walked out.

Just what is the HDR model? It's being truthful...

And it's simple. In fact, it's so simple, you'll ask yourself "Why didn't I think of that?"

HDR Model

Honest—Being *truthful* about your thoughts and feelings

Direct—Being *truthful* in simple and straight-forward terms

Respectful—Being *truthful* without blaming, confronting, or trying to control

THAT'S IT!

So, how does it work?

- Being *honest* has to be a measured response—one that will be understood in the context of the situation: you won't tell the folks at a pharmacy conference that you feel deeply hurt by their action, for example, although you might say that to one of your children or another family member. At the conference, I measured the audience and said I felt distracted and upset.

- Being *direct* means you tell the truth in simple and straightforward terms. It was very, very difficult for me as a passive person to be direct. I would beat around the bush and observe people looking at me with a puzzled expression, wondering "What is he talking about?"
- Being *respectful* means telling the truth without blaming; explaining something in an objective way; reporting not reacting.

> HDR is not confronting,
> it's becoming a truth teller.

It's coming from a place of strength, it's not about controlling.

I had an experience at work where someone was very angry with me about a decision I made, and said something very negative about me to a group of employees. The first thing I wanted to do was *defend myself*. Then, I thought, what would it look like to come from a place of strength in this situation? As I walked up to the group, they all looked at me; my co-worker was apparently still upset, and asked me, "Why did you do that? Why did you make that decision?"

I asked her if she would like to discuss this alone with me, in private, but she declined.

I then replied, *"Have you already made up your mind or would you like to hear from me?"* (That's an HDR skill—and it's a phrase that you can memorize.) My first impulse was to walk up and start defending myself—but down deep, I knew I should come from a place of strength, and not try to gain power or defend myself.

Because of my response, the person said in a frustrated way, "OK, I really do want to hear from you."

I began to explain, and after not more than 30 seconds, she began to scream and yell at me. I stopped, and in an honest, direct and respectful way said, "I'm a little confused right now. A minute ago, you said you wanted to understand why I made that decision. Now, you're talking loudly and you are in my face, and I wonder, do you really want to hear from me?"

She said, "No, I don't want to hear from you."

I went back to my office, and later several employees came by and said they admired the way I handled things. Although I didn't confront her about her behavior, I was able to gain resolution because I came from a place of strength. I couldn't control her, but I controlled myself. A few days later, she came to me and we were able to obtain some resolution to the situation.

But how do you make it work?

The important thing is to *just begin using the HDR model* to the best of your ability. There's a saying in addictions groups: "Fake it until you make it." You may feel like you're "faking" it at first, but as you understand your bent (passive, reactive, or TOP), and learn to move to a middle place by consciously choosing to be honest, direct and respectful, you'll find it becomes a part of you.

The result of HDR

HDR will give you a new way to look at your life and communication style and build your sense of self-worth, not by confronting others or measuring yourself by them, but simply measuring yourself to your own response as a human being.

By being honest, direct and respectful.

MAKING IT WORK FOR YOU...

1. On a scale of 1-10

- How truthful are you when expressing your thoughts and feelings?
- How truthful are you about being straight-forward?
- Are you truthful without confronting, blaming or trying to control?

2. Think about a family member, neighbor, or co-worker with whom you have difficulty communicating; this week, how might you respond to them in an honest, direct, and respectful manner?

How to be Honest, Direct, and Respectful

Bringing It Into Focus

I once had a very passive client who worked as a loan processor. Joe was a hard worker; one day he told me he was quitting his job. "Why?" I asked.

He told me about the previous day: "A group of 15 of us were working together; the manager came by and threw a file on my desk and told me, 'I want this done by the end of the day.'" Clearly stressed, Joe said to me, "I can't take it anymore."

I replied, "I've encouraged you to be honest, direct and respectful with your manager for a long time. Would it hurt to talk to her?

You're going to quit anyway." I continued, "I'd like to see you walk away coming from a place of strength, by telling her how her behavior affected you. Tell her you're choosing not to be a victim anymore—just don't be confrontational and go down to her level."

So, we worked on clarifying the event and practiced how he would talk with her.

"Now, what was her original behavior?" I asked him.

"She was rude to me," he responded.

"Was that a behavior or your interpretation?"

"That's an interpretation," he replied.

"What did she do?"

"Well, she came into my office and threw the file on my desk," he explained.

"That's it?" I asked. "How did you feel?"

"I felt embarrassed, frustrated, like crawling under my desk," he admitted. "It made me wonder if she appreciates the fact that I'm one of the highest producers in the office."

So Joe and I practiced, and he went in to work the next day—the day he was going to quit. When his boss arrived, he told her, "I'd like to talk to you."

"Really? What do you want to tell me?" she asked.

He replied, "When you came in and threw the file on my desk and demanded, 'I want this done by the end of the day,' in a loud voice in front of everyone, I felt embarrassed, I felt hurt, and I felt disappointed, and it made me wonder if you know how hard I work to be the top producer."

Joe called me on the phone afterwards and said, "I did it!" and then he said, "Aren't you going to ask what happened?"

"It's not that I don't want to know what happened—it's just that I'm more excited you were able to come from a place of strength," I replied.

He told me anyway. "She looked at me and said, 'You're absolutely right. I've been under a lot of stress and pressure at home and at work, and I took it out on you. To show you I appreciate you, I'm going to give you the rest of the day off with pay'."

Being honest, direct, and respectful brings your message "into focus" so you can communicate clearly and move toward resolution.

When we have conflict in our lives, we usually want—and need—some sort of resolution to it. That can come in one of two ways:

1. External—we talk it out, understand underlying issues, and resolve it.
2. Internal—some people are so closed and protective, they won't respond well to what you say. But if you handle it from a "place of strength" way, an HDR type of way, you can feel some kind of internal resolution.

Remember, in your attempt at resolution,

76

it's perfectly acceptable to have an unexpressed thought. One of the most difficult things for me was to realize that I don't have to share everything that runs across my mind. There are times when it's important to let go and say, "I have enough internal strength and integrity not to have to take on this battle." That's a totally different situation than just going to the passive place.

Putting HDR into practice: so, what's a focus message?

A focus message has one goal—being truthful with yourself and the other person for the purpose of resolution and/or letting go. It's just one way to put HDR into practice.

Many people have been to seminars where they have learned about "I" messages. In my practice, I began to modify the "I" message—adding, deleting, and taking away some of the elements. One day, I was working with an intern therapist who was in training, and I referred to the modified "I" message; she stated: "I call them a *focus message* with my clients, *because it brings what I want to say into focus.*" As soon as she said it, I realized it was really a better name.

These messages help bring things into focus. It's a little like going to a movie where the film is out of focus—it's distracting, and keeps you from focusing on the movie.

A lot of the ways we communicate distract people and take the focus off what we really want to say, or what we want people to hear.

Contents of a focus message

There are three parts to giving a focus message:

1. Identify the person's *behavior.*
2. Identify *my feeling about the behavior.*
3. Identify *what I want, wish, or wonder.*

Then, STOP. Don't say any more!

How to put it into practice...

In a focus message, we begin by saying, **"when you,"** because we are *paying attention to the person's behavior,* not our interpretation of their behavior. This is a very important distinction to make!

For example, if I said to someone, "I was upset because you were *rude* to me today," that is my interpretation of a behavior. But, if I say to them instead, "I was upset **when you** *told me I was worthless,*" that would be naming—or identifying—the behavior.

1. Identify the behavior

Say what the person actually did, not your interpretation of what they said or did. If I said, "You gossiped about me today," that's my interpretation of the behavior. But, if I said, "You told Joe something I shared with you in confidence," I'm naming the behavior—I'm saying what you actually did.

One way I can identify the behavior is by making the statement

"When you…"

2. Identify the feeling
This needs to be a measured response depending on who you're speaking to. You would identify a deeper level of feeling with a loved one than you would with a co-worker, for example.

Avoid using the word, "like." (I feel *like* you're attacking me). As soon as you say, "I feel like," you won't say what you really feel, you'll probably say something along the line of, "I feel like you're an idiot" or "I feel like you're attacking me." Instead, say…

"I feel…"
and then name the feeling: I feel sad,
I feel happy, I felt discouraged
(it's also perfectly acceptable to use a focus
message to share something positive).

It's important when identifying feelings to understand that anger may not be a feeling. In most cases, the feeling underneath the reaction of anger is hurt or fear. (We will address this in the next chapter.)

3. Identify what I want, wish or wonder
Identifying what "I want " is usually done with children or if you're in a management position; with a child or employee, if you tell them what you don't want, it's important to also tell them what you do expect from them.

The "I wonder" has to do with a continuation of my feeling… "It makes me wonder if you appreciate the work I've done here;" "It makes me wonder if you really love me;" "It makes me wonder if you thought about my feelings before you made that decision."

The "wish" part is a way of letting someone know what you want without telling them to do it. "I wish you would be more expressive with your feelings;" "I wish you would tell me you love me more;" "I wish you would think of my needs before your own."

Here's another example:

Remember the story about the pharmacy convention at the start of Chapter Six? This was my focus message to the folks at the table who were talking.

1. When you: First, I identified the behavior (not my interpretation of it)

As I thought about the behavior of that "table of talkers" my first thought was that they were rude. But is that a behavior? No, it's my interpretation of a behavior. When I was giving my seminar their behavior was: **they were talking**. And in this case, there were two behaviors. The second was when I paused, **they got louder**.

2. I feel/felt: I identified my feeling and measured it

At this point, I shared a very low level feeling with them: **I felt distracted**.

"When I was giving the seminar and you folks were talking, I was really **distracted**. When I looked at you and you continued to talk louder, I was **upset and frustrated**."

3. It makes me wonder, wish or want: I told them what I wanted:

"I hope you don't treat other speakers the way you treated me tonight." And then I stopped.

What I did was come from a place of strength. And as I walked out the door of the ballroom I yelled "Yes!"

The life changing part of HDR is saying, "I'll fake it till I make it."

The "making it" part is having a sense of personal respect and integrity; it's coming from a place of strength, and not trying to control people.

In retrospect

If I had **reacted** to the talkers in Chapter Six would they have heard me? No, they would have focused on my delivery and said, "Wow! That guy's a hothead. He talked about stress and just look at him!"

If I had been **passive** and ignored it, I would have suffered as a result. *They* probably wouldn't have felt anything, and wouldn't have been challenged about their behavior.

I felt part of my responsibility was to challenge them for the benefit of other speakers and myself.

What happened next?

I've told this story at hundreds of seminars, and people always ask, "What did they (the talkers) do?"

I'll admit, it wasn't important to me what they did, because at that point *I had internal resolution.* In the past, I would have taken their behavior and everything else that happened that day and been a grump in a reactive way when I got home. I would have been destructive to others and maybe even to myself.

Or, I might have stopped and bought a box of Twinkies, thinking that would make me feel better.

So, what *did* the talkers do after I spoke to them? Nothing.

They sat and stared as I walked out of the room.

Two days later, though, I got phone calls from some of them—they went through a lot of trouble to find my personal number so they could apologize.

That was the icing on the cake. Rather than respond, as the passive person that I am, 'Oh, that's OK." I said. "I really appreciate the call and I accept your apology."

HONEST—DIRECT—RESPECTFUL

I always tell this story at my seminars, and when I finish, I always ask: "Was I honest, direct, and respectful?" and the audience always says "Yes."

Someone once said to me, "It would be so much easier if I could be honest and direct, and didn't have to be respectful!"

Would it?

Honest, Direct and Respectful is a grid to measure

my response in any situation

Focus Message

When you _____
(name behavior – don't interpret)

I feel _____
(how do you feel – don't say "like...")

and I want,
wish or
wonder _____

THEN STOP!!!

MAKING IT WORK FOR YOU...

1. Think of a challenging situation, when having a focus message would have been a help to you.
2. Fill in the blanks to create that focus message:

When you: _____

I feel: _____

And I:

Want: _____

Wish: _____

Wonder: _____

The Personal Side of HDR

The Sensitive Side—When the Past Affects the Present

I had been working with a patient for many months when I jokingly said, "Now that you're getting your life back together you might want to cut your hair." (You have to understand I was trying to be funny—I am always jealous of people who still have hair.)

Suddenly, he became furious and started yelling obscenities at me.

My first response was to defend myself. Then, I stopped and said, "I'm really sorry, I don't know what I said that made you so angry; I want to assure you I didn't intend to."

He stopped yelling and replied, "When I was 14 years old my dad held a gun to my head and made me cut off all my hair."

That event had created a sensitivity that had stayed with him all these years—and I had hit that sensitivity without realizing it.

Now, I understood his anger and felt empathy for him—and was truly sorry for what I had said.

It's important to understand that things from our past can get in the way of effectively implementing the HDR model:

- dealing with hurt, anger and bitterness.
- our sensitivities (those things that 'push our buttons').
- our belief systems and their effect on our lives.

THE PERSONAL SIDE OF HDR

Things that get in the way...

Dealing with hurt, anger and bitterness

In our culture, we're taught that anger is a legitimate feeling. But I've come to believe it's almost always a *reaction* to the feelings of hurt and fear. If I can help people understand they are angry, and then lead them back to the underlying hurt and fear, that's where they will find internal resolution and, through forgiveness, the potential for reconciliation.

I was working in counseling with a girl, 16, and her father, and I had trained them in the HDR model so we could have a way to measure communication. They were trying to become closer by being honest, direct and respectful with each other.

They were fairly new to the counseling process. One day they came in and the father immediately began to yell and scream about his daughter's behavior.

He said, "I can't believe what you're doing and the crowd you're hanging out with—can't you see what you're doing?" He was filled with blame and anger.

"How do you feel?" I asked the dad.

"I feel angry," he said.

I said, "That is not a feeling."

"I know, it's hurt or fear!" he threw back.

"So, which one is it?" I said.

He didn't say anything. He just sat there, with big tears running down his face, and finally said, "I'm so afraid and so hurt by the way she's living her life." And he just sat there and wept.

His daughter turned and looked at him...and I saw an amazing transformation take place in the session.

As long as we had focused on his anger, we couldn't get below to the hurt and fear.

What he was saying—beneath the blame and anger—was, "When you do these things, I feel so hurt, and so afraid, and it makes me wonder if you'll ever be able to turn around, come back, and be a part of the family."

Sensitivities

What happens when you go to the dentist and, while working on your teeth, she hits a sensitive spot? You yell! You don't stop and say, "Oh, you've hit a spot that is quite tender."

Sensitivity is an instantaneous reaction. The only way we can learn not to react is to desensitize something. How? By putting things in a proper perspective and coming to grips with what it really means.

Think about that boy with the long hair at the start of this chapter. The sensitivity over my comment wasn't going to go away—it had been there for a long time—but then I was able to put it into perspective: first, that I wasn't his dad and second, that having someone hold a gun to your head and tell you to cut off all your hair means you are powerless and worthless and don't count for anything...those are things we have to challenge when we're starting to get really honest and get really direct and get really respectful. The trouble comes from the meaning we attach to those beliefs, thoughts and feelings.

Belief systems and their affect on our lives

Belief systems affected my life in a significant—and often detrimental—way. For one thing, my dad and my brothers were mechanical guys. I was more of a people person; I can remember really getting angry when I tried to fix things.

One day, I realized this was a huge sensitivity that made me feel inadequate. I had been given an Erector Set at an early age, and I realized I didn't want to play with it—it wasn't my thing. At seven years of age, I'd rather be at my neighbor's, talking with the family. As I grew up, I didn't accept the part of myself that wasn't mechanical and I began to understand the meaning I attached to this sensitivity: I thought all men were mechanical and, since I wasn't mechanical, I wasn't a man.

When I got in situations where I needed to fix things, I'd react with anger—but underneath the anger I felt hurt and fear. And you know, those sensitivities never go away. But they can be managed if you learn to challenge them and put them in a proper perspective.

What I learned from the spa

When I decided to put a spa in my backyard, I was smart enough to realize I needed someone to help me—so I got help. As the installer was hooking up the spa, he turned to me and said, "Do you have any seal tight conduit?"

I said, "No," and he asked me to go to the hardware store to get some.

So I went down, and asked a salesperson where the seal tight conduit was. He said, "It's over in the plumbing section."

I said, "I don't know what it looks like, could you help me find it?"

He then yelled, as loud as he could, "YOU DON'T KNOW WHAT SEAL TIGHT CONDUIT IS?"

Even though I had processed that sensitivity and understood where it came from, I felt all those same old feelings coming back. Part of me wanted to walk away and be passive, and the other part wanted to be sarcastic and really put him in his place.

But what I said was, "I do a lot of things well, but mechanical things are not one of them, and I really need your help."

Not only did he help me find it, he became a friend and helped me finish installing the spa.

If I hadn't understood and adequately dealt with my sensitivity, I wouldn't have understood my communication style…and I would have, once again, made a mess of things.

__HDR Cycle__

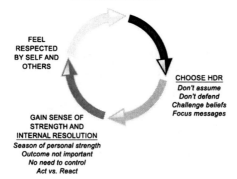

TENSION / ANGER / STRESS

FEEL
RESPECTED
BY SELF AND
OTHERS

CHOOSE HDR
Don't assume
Don't defend
Challenge beliefs
Focus messages

GAIN SENSE OF
STRENGTH AND
INTERNAL RESOLUTION
Season of personal strength
Outcome not important
No need to control
Act vs. React

HDR only works if we are committed to

personally understanding our sensitivities and

understanding that others have sensitivities also.

MAKING IT WORK FOR YOU...

1. Think about what you are most "sensitive" about. How does this interfere with your ability to relate to others?

2. What is the most recent example of your sensitivity? How did it interfere with your ability to practice HDR?

3. How many times have you defended yourself in the last week? Think of one situation:

   - Did it help?

   - How did it hurt?

   - How could you have handled things differently?

   - How would you have felt then?

The Incredible Result of HDR

I've seen countless lives and even corporate
cultures change through people using the
principles of HDR. At one company, when I
first arrived as the manager, people didn't talk to
each other—they talked about each other. I kept
saying, "Let's not talk about people, let's talk to
them."

As a result of learning and practicing HDR,
people began to talk with each other to resolve
differences and difficulties. In time, the admin-
istration worked the principles of being honest,
direct and respectful into every employee's
annual review.

Sitting around in a room and talking about people you don't like will never make you feel better, it will only cause you to feel worse, and it won't solve the problem.

Reacting strongly to a person who you feel hurt and anger toward for a given situation won't get you what you want, because people will focus on what you're doing and not what you're saying.

If you've ever gone fishing with a spinning reel, and gotten a big knot in the line, you understand the temptation to just cut the line to get rid of the knot and start over. That's what some people do with their lives: they leave a job, leave a marriage or other relationships rather than say, "I'll try and untangle that knot."

HDR will help you untangle those knots. It will give you a new way to look at your life and communication style and build your sense of self-worth, not by confronting others or measuring yourself by them, but simply measuring yourself to your own response as a human being...

   ...by being honest, direct and respectful.

SAY IT...

Honest
Direct
Respectful

For more information or to schedule a speaking engagement, please contact Dennis at: info@hdrsolutions.com

Visit his website at www.hdrsolutions.com

CPSIA information can be obtained
at www.ICGtesting.com
Printed in the USA
FFOW05n0737141016